Feb 2, 2007

The
New
Year
of
Yellow

Ford, Amanda & Eliott-

It gives me the greatest joy to share this book w/ you, the friendship, this very odd & lonely time in our lives. I (Rachel & Elinna too) am so glad that you are in our lives!

Enjoy!

Mark Jay

The New Year of Yellow

Matthew Lippman

Winner
of the 2005
Kathryn A. Morton
Prize in Poetry
Selected by
Tony Hoagland

Sarabande Books
LOUISVILLE, KENTUCKY

Managing Editor
Sarabande Books, Inc.
2234 Dundee Road, Suite 200
Louisville, KY 40205

Library of Congress Cataloging-in-Publication Data

Lippman, Matthew, 1965–
    The new year of yellow : poems / by Matthew Lippman.— 1st ed.
        p.   cm.
    ISBN 1-932511-46-6 (pbk. : alk. paper)
    I. Title.
    PS3612.I647N49 2007
    811'.6—dc22   2006004405

ISBN-13: 978-1-932511-46-8

Cover image: *Blue/Yellow (small),* 2004. Oil on wood panel, with stones, by Kate Hammett. Provided courtesy of the artist.

Cover and text design by Charles Casey Martin

Manufactured in Canada
This book is printed on acid-free paper.

Sarabande Books is a nonprofit literary organization.

THE KENTUCKY ARTS COUNCIL

The Kentucky Arts Council, a state agency in the Commerce Cabinet, provides operational support funding for Sarabande Books with state tax dollars and federal funding from the National Endowment for the Arts, which believes that a great nation deserves great art.

For Rachel

Contents

Part III

Acknowledgments

These poems have appeared
or will appear in the
following journals:

The American Poetry Review	"Mid-Afternoon Shut-Eye," "South Going South"
Conduit	"The Joy Is Everywhere"
Diagram	"And Everywhere It's Florida"
Fence	"Apple Psalm"
Forklift: Ohio	"Made of Something," "Thataboy"
Hayden's Ferry Review	"I Suppose the Sadness of Things"
Indiana Review	"Raising Ali"
The Iowa Review	"The New Year of Yellow"
The Literary Review	"Where the Hand Meets the Expectation of the Hand," "The Camouflage of 4/4 Time"
Lyric	"My Austrian Buick"
Margie	"Of Nazareth"
Pleiades	"Blonde and All," "Storming the Boardwalk"
Seneca Review	"Hallelujah Terrible," "Valentine's Day"
Spinning Jenny	"Moby Toby," "The Art of Being Backward," "A Few a Day"
Witness	"Señor His Spatula" (originally published as "Not the Millennium")

9

"Hallelujah Terrible" appeared in *The Best American Poetry 1997*.

"Thataboy" won Honorable Mention in the Los Angeles Poetry Contest, 1999.

I would like to extend my gratitude to the James A. Michener/Paul Engle Poetry Fellowship for its assistance in making this book possible.

GRATITUDES

I would like to thank my family for all their love and support—Mel, Carol, Amy, Maria, Rebecca, Gary, Anna, Anita, Nomi, Sharky, and Billy;

friends and readers—Michael Morse for every sky we've ever shared, Mark Bloom for being around the corner for twenty-nine years, Gary Shapiro for his endless wisdom and fortitude, Scott Segal, Mark Heyert, Lisa Hacken, Thaddues Russell, Rose Greenberg, Dr. Linda Marcus, Deborah Tall, Beth Harrison, Adam Bohannon, Kevin Prufer, René Steinke, David Bonanno, Matt Hart, all my students at Roslyn High School, Sarah Gorham, Kirby Gann, Kristina McGrath, Nickole Brown, Jeannette Pascoe, and all the wonderful folks at Sarabande, and Tony Hoagland for his benevolence and faith in these poems, for giving them a road to roam in this one, small world, and for saying *yes;*

and most dearly—to Rachel for all her deep love and guidance and to Eliana, for breaking our hearts wide open each and every day.

Foreword

Call me a Pollyanna but I secretly believe that everyone knows the mind of poetry. Maybe only down in the subtle tissues of the pineal gland, or the appendix of childhood, perhaps only dimly, perhaps not often, but they remember. Everyone has had a taste of it somewhere along the line. Somewhere deep inside their neural Wyoming, they know what poetry is. And to have a taste is to want another taste. "This is the best they is, the best forever," says one of the characters in one of these poems, and that's the truth the sweet spot knows. It's also a foundational truth of Matthew Lippman's poetry—that ebullience is a part of the human condition, that imagination is guaranteed by the Constitution. That faith in the available redemption of joy is what most makes me trust this poetry, and makes me believe that an army cadet or a corporate attorney might take this book off a shelf in a waiting room, open it, and laugh.

This coming from a guy who hasn't had sex in a really long time.
Well, had sex five weeks ago, once, with a woman in another state
and it was like visiting The Planetarium.
Fascinating
but you don't go back for another seven years. . . .
That was me in a nutshell yesterday
after the joy was in my knees
and my eye twitched for hours.
I'll tell you, not having sex is a waltz all by itself.
And then all your married friends say,

It's a draft from under the door, sex.
What do they mean?....

("The Joy Is Everywhere")

Different poets possess different powers. So Lippman has eros and humor; somehow, also, he has a great, unfalsifiable affection for human nature. But his work is also empowered by verbal gusto, a faith in the joy of saying. As my friend Ed says, "There are grownups and then there are poets." Lippman teaches high school kids, yet often he seems as manic and transgressive as one of his own teenage students. He respects both fantasy as well as honesty, he understands both bluntness and evasion, crying and flying. His speaker moves back and forth from hard truths to nuttiness:

What I did, I lied.
I lied about the Cremora Food truck hijacked,
brought to Boston,
blown up,
just to get all that white powder up in the air,
just to get the kids to listen;

I lied about the money and the hungry zookeeper
who killed two giraffes with a bullhorn
then wheeled out the hibachi....

("And Everywhere It's Florida")

Just as Lippman is not afraid to use fantasy as a defense against reality, he regularly serves up a sobering dose of hard truth as anodyne against silliness and triviality.

> Sometime at the end of the 1980s the Holocaust closed down for me.
> It might have been after a conversation I had with Lia Purpura at
>   the Foxhead
> over a couple of Dubuque Stars
> but I think it was more of a gradual finalé,
> mowing lawns, leaky sinks,
> a few jobs, a few cars.
> And then one day it was over,
> the entire fascination,
> the almost desire to have been in it, part of it,
> part of something. . . .
>
> Imagine such a desire,
> to be in *that*. . . .
>
> ("Gave Up the Holocaust")

In their aspect of worldliness, Lippman's poems are peopled, and one of the true pleasures of *The New Year of Yellow* is the way that the citizens talk to each other. To me perhaps the pithiest summation of this book's mission in the world occurs in the poem "Valentine's Day," when someone says:

It's not the same anymore, the way the painters paint.
Nobody wants to show the body.
Nobody wants to touch themselves enough to know there is a body.

But that's not true of our poet. And because he does touch himself, in the brazen and humble tradition of Gerald Stern and Frank O'Hara and Whitman, because he dares to, we are given to remember our bodies, the body of the world, and the spirit which moves around unpredictably inside it.

Full of exuberance and invention, flush with the stuff of struggle in the world, bright colored with mood, *The New Year of Yellow* is a defense of human nature. I believe in its animal instinct, its god-sanctioned, oxygen-breathing, self-evident inalienable right to pronounce:

> which is why I drop everything—
> my keys, my coat, my pants and t-shirt—
> and begin to dance on the side of the road,
> cars and donkeys and rickshaws and bicycles whiz past,
> dance this dance I've made up—all arms and ass—
> because I refuse,
> refuse refuse
> to go through the rest of these days thinking that I have wasted
>   anything.

("Insurrection")

—Tony Hoagland

Part I

Thataboy

I got fat.

I don't know how it happened.

I opened my pants one day

and a whole mess of stuff fell out.

One day my jowls were zeppelins and my hands floated to the ceiling.

I have enjoyed myself all the way to this fat spot—steaks and onions,

platters of shrimp in a nice cocktail,

some twenty-four thousand raviolis in fra diavlo.

What did it say about the world, my fat?

The guy down the block looked at me and said, *only in America.*

Goddamn right, I replied, *go Bulldogs.*

It was another in a slew of exhibitions that I had learned to put on

to keep myself from feeling slim.

When my buddy Mike called from the car-phone

he told me he was headed down the road for a couple of cheeseburgers at
   McDonalds.

Thataboy.

We've always been on the same page like that.

Americans with a taste for a rack of ribs when the goings get tough

and somewhere out there in the green pastures

our mothers are feeling the hurt of another herd of violent men.

It's a thought, you know, that we kept ourselves from inheriting the rage
   of our fathers

by dipping into the Hollandaise.

That's what I'll name my son to keep him from destroying the women that he will take to the dances.

I'll name him Hollandaise.

Hollandaise, go do your homework.

Hollandaise, go talk to your mother.

I got a ways to go before that.

Tonight it's biscuits and gravy with a side of pork the Iowa farmer sent

from the middle of Iowa

just to make sure we get our USDA stamp of approval

on getting big.

Surf Buddha

There is a sandalwood Buddha on the desk that has my stomach
and I don't suppose to call myself a Buddha
or even pretend to know much about Buddhist whirlings
but Rachel gave me the thing and it's got my belly
the one my father has
and the one his father had
and I know this bulge the way I know my name,
and can't believe I've become the language of fat
that the boys in my family have kept quiet.

So I encourage my stomach out into the world,
rub it on a daily basis and think
that if I ever become a religious man
there would be god and glory to find there,
my rib cage distended,
my love of ice cream as sweet as my love of Rachel

who put the Buddha in my palm a month after we met and said, *have this*,
and I said, *I already have this*,
my hands in motion around my bellybutton and then today
noticed for the first time that the little bastard has got some serious
    nipples on him,
thank god, and breasts too,
he's the perfect kind of godlike statuette
even if I am a Jew

but the days have been glorious and people die in truck crashes

and men beat their wives and flowers bloom purple

and the cardinal I've named Jack always comes around my way at this time,

4:40 in Baldwin on the Island,

Wes Montgomery on the Sony

and I don't know if it's his song *Cariba* or the wind on my swollen toes

that makes me pick up the little guy, stick him in my mouth,

swirl him around between teeth and cheek,

place him on the edge of my tongue and let him surf there,

through the neighborhood of my white heat,

on the curl of my pink waves.

And Everywhere It's Florida

What I did, I lied.
I lied about the Cremora Food truck hijacked,
brought to Boston,
blown up,
just to get all that white powder up in the air,
just to get the kids to listen;

I lied about the money and the hungry zookeeper
who killed two giraffes with a bullhorn
then wheeled out the hibachi.

I lied about living rooms on fire
and dead cowboys on my lawn
who rode clean out of thin air
before I shot 'em with my six gun
cried *Geronimo,*
broke down in hives
and got lost in the Hollywood tumbleweed.
All my life it's been helicopter blades in my spine;
all my life I've lied.

When I was six I didn't believe there were frogs in the pond and lied that
    there were,
green ones with red tongues,

ones with poisonous venom that might bite me in butt,
turn me into a ragged prince.

At fifteen I lied about my hair,
that it was short and clean
and that I was headed for the Marines
to become a three-star general
then kick some serious ass in places I didn't even know existed,

like Tahoe,

go to Tahoe and mow the bastards down
in their ski-boot delirium,
their bunny-suit pirouette.

What I did,
I lied about hearing voices and nailing myself to a cross;
I lied about the visiting team and about the French Revolution,
that it happened on Suez soil
and that we live for love
then die alone.

Maybe I didn't lie about that,
maybe that's all there is when the hotcakes come,
a slab of butter,
a busty waitress name Charlene with the short skirt and large lips
and everywhere it's Florida.

I've been there once, I can't tell a lie,
to visit my grandmother.
Then she died;
I didn't go to the funeral, what I did,
I stayed home and watched t.v.

Storming the Boardwalk

Mike takes the F-train to Coney Island to sit on the beach and smoke a
    joint.
It's Thursday afternoon.
He's got a book by Calvino in his pocket,
a book about vanishing.
When I talk to him later
he tells me he doesn't think he can take much more of this city living.
I want a cabin in Maine with trees, he says.
You can have the trees, I say, *but forget the rest.*
And downtown his woman is stranded.
She doesn't know what he knows about Coney Island,
that it sinks into the sea like Venice
and then rises from the sea *not* like Venice.
The whole thing is one big sea-saw
that might catapult him gone
and one big fleet of submarines lurks off the Brooklyn shore from the 40s
when all the little boys had GI uniforms and stormed the boardwalk.
Ivan and Mel took Brighton Beach in forty seconds flat when they were
    eight
and the Italians meant nothing.
Calvino was elsewhere
digging potatoes out of the brain of some Nazi clopper he'd capped in
    the heart with a Luger
while 3000 miles away The Cyclone ripped everyone's hair out
and left them peeing from laughter.

Mike wants none of it on his little day trip down to the beach
with a bag of cheap sensimilla and that book on disappearing.
If I could he wonders—disappear that is—
I'd be a tree without a century and a birth without a cord;
I'd walk through hours of azaleas and turn a corner.
But the herb has him and the cackle of the distant F
and the waves breaking,
the slosh of ocean water up against ageless and yellow sand
as he watches the boardwalk for his Russian wife, Natasha,
and that those submarines
with their *up periscope* power
will come rescue him from the salt.
He sits and watches for Calvino in his broken-down car;
for Ivan and Mel, young, victorious and green;
and for the still waters in his veins that will finally send him home.

Noodles

(for Mark Bloom)

Hey Noodles,
what's up with the noodles?
Hear they've gone up four cents in Lanzhou
and you down in Little Chinatown,
with your Red Sea Scroll manifestos,
with your adolescent shadows
and all your high school pals dipping the back end of tomorrow
into bowls of beef broth and bok choy
just to remember the name of the first Suzie
you drove home after midnight
through the flower-rain of a late afternoon.

In Lanzhou the noodles are up a couple of mao
and down at my local geisha joint
you can get a bowl of udon with chicken for fifteen bucks.
That's the difference between Asia and New York,
the color of flesh.
But Noodles, I won't tell if you won't.

You beefed-up Jew with your lo mein agita and wannabe gangster tallit
wielding nightingales for sunshine.

The trouble with China, the way I see it,
is if you're making ninety dollars a month wielding noodles,
whose gonna notice when the pollution gets so bad

there's no air to suck up through the nostrils
when you've got a bowl of chow fun in your face
and you're doing the slurp?

Noodles, I wrote you a postcard from Lanzhou yesterday.
I was with my peddler's stick and lost between two worlds.
I said, Hey Noodles,
I miss your noodles,
the ones you used to serve up when we were twelve,
that pasta sauce with a dash of dill,
that way we used to get it all over the floors for fun.

I said, Lanzhou needs a man like you to clean up the mess,
get all these poor folk fattened up.

You Noodles,
to open up a joint called *Noodles' Noodles*
and save the entire mainland of China
with your hot steaming bowls of kreplach,
your soba with scallions,
your chow mein with the spicy chicken.

Where the Hand Meets the Expectation of the Hand

The ten-year-old boy with his tube socks rolled up to his knees—
in The Pine Woods of dances and singing
and then campfires with sparkling pieces of wood rising through the trees
to meet the sparkling pieces of gas
that science teachers all over the world call gas,
but which he believed to be the headlights of busted-down cars
with their brights on
waiting to be rescued.
He feels mosquitoes through his skin
and smacks them if he can get them
because there is that thing about blood
which he has always had
especially when it is his own.
Who could tell him anything different except Deb with her perfect long
    black hair,
that blood was just a flower that they could call strawberries
when they were older.
And later, when he gets older,
he'll ask himself how he knew back then
what beauty was
and how it came to be her.
He was ten
burning as he ran with sticks down to the river,
marshmallow caked to this side of his lips

with pine needle sap whirling around in there like gases whirling around
	out there.
His man Jack wanted to crawl through the ferns on a mission
through the brush for enemy fighters
as the guitar and banjo duet up the hill
finally got them in that sad place
that all ten-year-old boys have
to save them from just this sort of reconnaissance.
It forced him to his feet and he walked to the campfire and sat closer to
	himself
than perhaps he had ever sat before
leaving Jack to be near Deborah.
He thought he would try and save one of those cars tonight if he could
by mustering up the earth in his left hand to hold her right
in that way that hands are that one thing
and gases the other.

Blonde and All

I want a blonde.
A real blonde.
A blonde with highheeled shoes and a necklace made of shells.
I want her with an American flag draped around her legs
and a Chevrolet in her veins.
Is it too much to ask, one Jew to the rest of the world?
Is it a dobro on the lap of a western man
or a city man falling off his curb before the bus even rounds the corner?

A blonde. I want a blonde.
I can't say where the desire comes from.
I go to the movies and the women fill the screen awash in lavender
with their blonde curls and their famous lips
and I think, If I could just sit in this chair long enough,
one will sit down next to me, put her tongue in my ear, swivel it around.
Then I will be a man from the gravel and the spit-shine
and I will be a man from the literati.
I will be the whole entire desire of the western world in one movie seat.
But until then, I'm just a Jew who wants a sweet blonde in jeans,
a blonde who rides horses and takes her time.
Give me a child I might say,
some child we can share like roasted peppers,
roasting up the sides of our bodies when we sleep
or when the fever runs high

or when the whole half of our sky goes from purple frost to
    godknowswhat.

Oh, it's all a ridiculous scheme I've cooked up in my head
about what this country really looks like out there.
It's a Cadillac Ranch kind of thing;
a Rockwell or a Campbell soup can without the Warhol kind of thing.
It's the far-side of me looking into the wrong peephole
and frankly I'm tired of figuring out the whole enterprise all at once
but can't imagine anything else, really,
except falling down on my own
into a little Japanese car that takes me out to the eastern end of the
    eastern tip
of my dark-haired and hazel-eyed self
while she falls down with me,
blonde and all.

Because I'm Black

When I ask Gerald why he's always in the hall
he says, *It's because I'm black.*
That's the joke around school these days:
why don't you do your homework?
It's because I'm black.
So I teach them that Emmett Till had a stutter the white man thought
    was a whistle
and wound up dead in the Tallahatchie River with a blown up head,
and that Stokely Carmichael's African name is Kwame Ture,
about lynchings and Malcolm X's piss and vinegar
and they say, hey mr. lipp, it don't mean anything anyway,
so I pull down the shades and scream *Spooky*
and no one understands
except the kid who reads her encyclopedia of American History
every night before she goes to sleep
so she can get into Duke or Williams
and says, *Lippman's a racist*
but I tell them I love everyone
and bring in James Brown records to explain groove
and Maria Callas arias to explain angelic
and Juan Felipe Herrera poems to explain to Alan Rodriguez
that the hood is the hood
no matter how many rhymed couplets you need
to get you off.
He says, *Yo lipp, you speak hispanic*

even though you a white-boy jew

and Daviece tells me to shut-up

and Zak looks like a migrant worker picking grapes

and Juliete has a silver stud jammed through her lip and wears

black rock band t-shirts every day, says,

It's because I'm black.

She's Sicilian and they all think that's a kind of pizza.

I'm paddling upstream here,

so I wear green pants and an orange shirt to school,

tell them I love Jamaicans who don't brush

and cowboys with long thumbs

and the sound of Spanish inside a Taco Bell,

and they call me a spook,

tell me I'm spooky,

ask me why I'm so short all the time.

And I have no choice but to sit down with my book on commas and tell
    them, Hey kids,

when you quote the text, put it before the quotation mark

even if you *are* black,

even if you feel that you're already a long way from home.

A Few a Day

I throw kids out of my classroom all the time.
I have to.
They bring in their submarines
and crash them into desktops,
blackboards.
They order pizza from Dominoes and blow up their homework.
I throw them out.

I tell them to get on the bus
take it down to Coney Island,
go for a walk,
smell the salt,
watch the juggler in a trench coat
ask for a dollar.

They don't listen.
It's a long-lasting battle.

Once,
Jackson with the big feet
talked me into canceling the exam on Milton and Proust.
He said: *I have my own memory of horror*
then proceeded to rip up the carpet with his knees.
I had to kick him out,
I had been duped.

He couldn't remember the first thing
about talking in rhyme.

When his aunt came in for a conference
she brought me a cake with a hacksaw in the middle.
Everything was all smiles and we laughed until we cried
and then all the windows broke.

It was the kids outside
throwing stones,
the ones I had already thrown out,
so I fetched the Drano.

That did nothing
and it was a week of Pound on Eliot
and Pound on Virgil
and Virgil walking happy through the autumnal sand.

Then I had to start throwing kids out again.
A few a day.
A couple before noon,
three after lunch.
But they all kept coming back
in their Sherman tanks
and their space shuttle detonations,
crashing full speed ahead
into the pictures on the walls
of Faulkner and Chaucer,

chalk dust in their eyes,
caterpillars who couldn't fly.

Come now, I said, *can't you see*
that your life is a fraction of a second too fast?

But they heard nothing and kept on talking
about satin robes and rabbit sex,
about razorblades and asbestos.

It was too much for any man steeped in physics and iambic
so I grabbed the back of my neck
to save the lesson

and hurled myself out of the classroom door
into the big sea
of this already exploding notebook.

Everyone Wants a Monkey

Everyone wants a monkey,

I can't afford them,

the orangutans, too much on the black market and even worse

at Bed Bath & Beyond;

my brother-in-law G. wants one with a Hasselblad strapped around its neck

shooting photos of the humans,

wants to put up a show downtown on the advancement of primates from
     the inside out.

I thought he was a genius

but the goddamn monkey was like fifteen thou;

then the shrink, kinda an animal herself, said one June day,

forget the bill,

you've been seeing me for twelve years and your big checks bore me,

get me a monkey,

she wanted a Great Ape from Africa,

one of those big suckers with a hairy butthole,

and I said,

but I don't got it in me,

she said, well, hasn't that always been the case.

And yesterday my buddy Mike came right out and said it too,

buy me a monkey,

dude wanted a certified primate from Senegal,

I said, man, how do you expect me to buy you a monkey from Senegal?

He said, forget about the money, steal the bastard from the Bronx Zoo,

I thought, has everyone gone mad,

has everyone checked out on me all at once?
I was in a quandary,
scratching my head with two fingers,
hanging from my tree with the other three.

My Austrian Buick

It's been a long time since the Socialists have invaded my life.

It's been a long time since I had a conversation about sharing the wealth

and waiting on line.

But then yesterday I was in the bookstore on 9th Street

when a woman with an Austrian accent

told me I should read more Max Jacob.

She was an odd-looking creature, shaped like a Buick,

and then we talked about living alone and maybe a little trip to Alaska.

I said, What does this have to do with the Socialists?

She replied, Trotsky made a mean cowboy if you knew how to ride him

    right.

Really? I said,

and wanted my whole life to be wrapped up in her life

because her hair was black and she looked like a Buick.

It had come to be that simple for me yesterday

after an existentialist haze that left me pondering my boys,

how I might raise them when I had them,

how they might turn out to be modern dancers or drag queens

or bulldozer operators on site.

I thought it would be cool to have a kid who ran a bulldozer

and whose mother was a Socialist.

That's what I thought when I stood in the poetry section with my

    Austrian Buick

and told her my mother fought in the revolution.

Oh yeah, she accented, which one?

The one with all the women in it, I replied,

and the one at the country house, on the verandah, overlooking the lake.

You know, that one with all the martinis.

I was in that one too, she said, when my mind was made up and I had
somewhere to go.

It was when I was a Socialist and everything was wrong.

And now you're a Buick, I thought, an Austrian Buick with beautiful
black hair.

You roll on and are widespread and raise Marx from the dead

with the lift of your tongue.

You do all these things, I thought, as I scanned the shelves for Max
Jacob's *Dice Cup*

because I needed to get somewhere quick.

And that's when she grabbed my hand

and ran me down the street to an ice-cream shop for a frappe

before we ran back to her house and made love in a chair

and whispered the name *Trotsky* after each and every kiss.

Part II

Girls Especially

Kids from Long Island have no mothers,
girls especially,
my friend Linda said on the porch
with a wad of Stilton jammed into her mouth.
But the ones from Syosset are the best
when they talk really loud
in front of themselves
no clothes on
at the iceberg lettuce mall.

I heard once that Walt Whitman
drove a tractor through a red barn,
screaming lungs,
naked.
Today he might want to blow up the shopping center
built in his name
with that big nuclear belly
or am I just thinking about myself again?

These kids from Merrick and Hewlett
wouldn't know how to amputate their arms and tongues
if you gave them a hacksaw and said,
Amputate your arms and tongues.

These kids don't know what the electricity has done to their mothers—
ripped them right off the beaches
into an intergalactic playground of face lifts,
of back-to-back boob jobs.

In four months it will be November,
and all the kids on Long Island want to talk about
is their hair and the color of their hair
and the way it all gets stuck between their teeth
when they floss with it
after five meals a day of radish and carrots.

Rabbits,
that's what I call them.
Today I called one *bitch*

and wanted to scour the earth to find her mother,
hook her up to the back of my tractor,
wild lungs, naked,
and drag her home
where the kids snack on crispers full of lettuce.

Don't you see, mammas,
they're lost to you and dying,
girls especially, oh yes,
the girls.

Insurrection

I want to get all liquored up on coffee
because the Brooklyn Queens Expressway was closed at 5:30 in the
    morning
and so I had to deek and bop my way through the backstreets
of Flatbush and East New York,
get my bony ass out to Long Island so I might
teach the kids about Hester Prynne's breastplate,
and it took me goddamn near two hours just to make it across
    the Nassau/Queens border,
James Wright, I thought, can go fuck himself with that *I've wasted my life*
    shit,
bloody sanitation truck overturned and all lanes closed;

then I hear Arafat's almost dead,
the election fixed
and what really gets me is the live interview with Kevin Sikes,
an NBC reporter in khakis calling from Fulluja
to say the firefight is fierce—
tank blasts going off in the background,
mortars every five seconds, machine gun rounds and grenades right there
    on my radio;

so I crash the car into a sycamore near the Roslyn Road exit to get my
    bearings,
stumble out of the vehicle and watch the thing explode

then walk east with my book-bag filled with no books
because I hate cars
and realize what does it matter if I'm late to school,
and who the hell wants to talk about Hester Prynne's sad face anyway?

which is why I drop everything—
my keys, my coat, my pants and t-shirt—
and begin to dance on the side of the road,
cars and donkeys and rickshaws and bicycles whiz past,
dance this dance I've made up—all arms and ass—
because I refuse,
refuse refuse
to go through the rest of these days thinking that I have wasted anything.

Where Are All the Puerto Ricans

I rode my bicycle through Bellingham
and all the poets were fascists
and my hair was pink
and I thought, this is not New York,
there are no Puerto Ricans.

I screamed,
Where are all the Puerto Ricans?

It was a scene out of Fellini
but there was an absence of Italian women

so I hit the town square
while the rain kept on in sheets
circled it and sang
and everyone was white;

Ah Christ, I screamed,
Where are they?

Then pedaled my green Schwinn
through hailstorms
and the foothills of Mt. Baker,
sped up and down the coast,

fought off grenade wielding, wild salmon
in search of Pedro,

a kid I knew once
who could graffiti an elevator door in thirty seconds

then slip outside till midnight
where his hairless chest burned firehouse red
like some ancient Aztecan god.

Oh God, I thought
where are you,

my brown-skinned compadré
and the flipped fingered hand-slap we invented
in a schoolyard daze,
two kids in the Columbus Avenue filth?

Where are you now, Pedro Gonzalez?
Stand up, I can't find you.

Señor His Spatula

across the way
the light goes out in my friend Señor's apartment
where each morning i see him cook eggs for his fourteen children packed
    in so tight
the walls are green from body spores
expelled in sleep
i see his light go out and wonder who i am
dropping my legs to the floor and thinking
at work they call me Matty when my name is Matthew
and short as i am
the stinking flowered sun
is at my fingertips each morning
when Señor lifts his head to grind up the eggs and get it going
so his children can have life in them like purple
or a memory of purple
i don't know anymore how any of us make it through the day
in our everyday underwear
soiling the world and having it rise at the same moment
when i pick up the orange or Señor his spatula
just to hum a little song
a little ditty for ourselves knowing damn well
the earth gets us every time and thank god

Excellent Still

I was six in '71,
and Diane Arbus' photo,
Stripper, San Francisco, 1968
destroyed me,

especially the dancer's pointer finger,
as it pushed softly against her right breast,
lifted it a bit,
the whole world a new pleasure in that bounce,
a plum;

so I lay on my bed for hours and knew it was good,
this woman and her manicured lust,
her perfect body
something else,

not an afternoon in the sandbox
or candy from Gus 'N' Bees,
but a world,
a universe of sweetness and horror
and that I might get there someday;

and I did,
with Natasha B.,
ten years later in Vermont under a sky of white birch,

she fell into me like waves against the sea
into my hands,
my mouth
said,
This is the best they is,
the best forever;

but it wasn't
and the Thetford sky went dark
and she turned away
the way youth urges us beyond
what is already before us;

and today, thirty-two years later,
I saw *Stripper* in a museum in San Francisco
with a thousand tourists
breathing down my neck,

that burlesque baby with the perfect breasts,
that long finger where it had been in 1968 and 1971,
excellent still;

I was six and thirty-eight all at once
so close to the ocean
my arms were flopped seals;

and all I could think about was
what Diane Arbus thought
after she swallowed the last of the little white pills—

her daughters Amy and Doon?
playground grenades?
her own breasts,
sagging like teats in middle age
in 1971?

In the multitudes alone
it was Diane Arbus and me
at six and thirty-eight and forty-eight,
me and Diane

as it was at the beginning and end
of two different narratives,
told and telling,
in the sweet mortuary blue
of 1971.

Apple Psalm

What Mike had to say,
that God was a delicious apple in November,
is what his other side said,
that you must eat yourself.
Meaning, that talking to an apple in your left hand on Broadway,
that you picked with your right hand in November,
is about as autumn as it gets.
Even if this leaves you with a bus ticket in your pants pocket to Hillsdale
after the first of December to live a little in snow
seasonally marching through Columbia County on its way out to sea.
Which is how God must have imagined it anyway—
that in this part of the Northern seaboard
most wind comes across Iowa first before Mike's got a chance to feel it on
    his hands.
Which is how God must have imagined the two sides of Mike in his
    brown camel hair
walking down Broadway with a picture of everyone outside him
moving in.

I Suppose the Sadness of Things

I suppose the sadness irks the fireman in the blue night sky that is the
    snow,
or made up by the snow,
the way snow can turn a whole entire street into a world of burning
    teevees
or just something orange
because his fires are never his
and he is always at a loss for them
when all the water hoses have been considered silent.

I suppose that if you were to ask the barrister who lives down at the end
    of the block
he might tell you that sadness for him is the same thing when his one lit
    candle is lit
in his brown and leathered library
as he peruses the legal books that did not make him famous.
What is it that gets me? he asks himself,
as the snow blows up against his tinted windows
when his upstairs-wife is upstairs waltzing in her cotton gown
just as the clock passes twelve-thirty.

I suppose too, that the little man called little man Max
who walks all alone to school when the yellow bus passes him at seven
and who is like a slow blown saxophone
has a sadness in him like a furnace.

Some days it keeps him warm and other days the repair guy has got to be
    called in
when the snow rolls over the plains
and the whole neighborhood is a freeze zone,
pipes busting and windows combusting up just to keep themselves warm.

And if all this is true, I suppose,
then calling out to a neighbor on the other side of his fence
to ask him how to jump start a mower in early spring
when the new wife has left to buy oranges for two dollars a pound
at the produce market near the post office
is how sadness can fall down inside of a man
like a big tree can fall down beside a man
when he's out on his lawn
figuring out how to pull the rip cord just to get it all started.

Mid-Afternoon Shut Eye

What do you do in the mid-afternoon
when all of your business has been taken care of
and there is only the nap?
Do you nap?
Do you risk the colliding of universes
when you wake from the small rest
or do you just wander from room to room whistling a song about
    construction
that your mother taught you when you were six
and had the tool belt on,
ready to go?
The choice is not clear
in the mid-afternoon
when 2nd Avenue blocks itself up with construction men ripping up pipe
that the city planners said: *rip up*.
The choice is never clear when to rest
except that rest is a moon on the water
that's been there forever.
And in that instance, when forever rises up out of its handheld grace,
you set yourself down between two pillows
in the work clothes you have had on for five days.
You set yourself down with a green bird on your shoulder
while the construction men on 2nd Ave. pull up the eighty-six- year-old steel
that's been rusting since you were six
and had the tool belt on

and were ready to go.
You pass them in their orange hats
and think about lending a hand—
but you've given all your hands away—
and say *adios*
like one brother to the next
like an orange cut in half—
one half ingested, the other, sitting on its blue plate
swelled in its own juice.

The Camouflage of 4/4 Time

What do you think about coffee
when you sit awake with a brush in your hand
and think the black man is the great institution of sorrow?
He's walking his way into your life
in the form of four fifteen-year-olds
who live on the other side of the tracks.
They say *sugardaddy* and *drugman*
and then in the absence of hell, in a pure moment of synthesis,
they say *blues*.
They say it in whispers to keep up the confusion
knowing both junctions and camouflaging the beauty of 4/4 time.
I can't figure out the two worlds either
when Albert Murray tells me that the real diaspora is the diaspora of ideas.
Before, a long time ago, he says,
there was no globe,
no circumnavigation of the mothership,
no time but the time in your head, in your small little town.
Afternoons were straw roofs turning aqua to amber
depending on the placement of the sun
or the sky without a sun.
Now, Africa is one second away
and I braid my own hair in tiny knots to untie what I know will either
    kill me
or make me forgivable.
The black man is my mother.

I see him in the eyes of the fifteen-year-old boys
raising the word *nigger* out of a new soil that is not ghetto or projects or
      cotton fields.
This earth is boys,
is Bentley and Tony and Ed and Everett with their tight arms reeling wild
simply trying to get a daddy out of a clean pair of pants.
Just git me a daddy, they say,
and everything looks confusing from here
even though there are falling stars for everyone,
there are terse moments between alleyways to instigate freedom.
I see it in my coffee cup before any of us can plug into the socket
and send out our answers, our demands,
the know-it-all-of-nothings we make up to get over and tolerate.
And Murray tells me there is no such thing as African hydraulics.
There are just hydraulics.
There is no such thing as a pure man,
we are always spying, stealing, masking, covering;
it is all sales.
They hock, we hock.
Even Bentley
in his chair
who whispers *blues* to me when I ask him the question about seeds,
of origins,
of Swing,
of the pure American ash of his finely tuned black skin called *horn*.

The Mouth of a Trumpet

When I saw Roy Hargrove rip out his own heart in the space that exists
between one's lips and the mouth of a trumpet
I thought my hands were going to remove themselves from my arms
and start dancing on the small table in front of me
which the patrons of the Village Vanguard have not replaced in over sixty years.

When I saw Roy Hargrove's dreadlocks drip over the slit of his eyes
I wondered if he was doing Horse the way Parker could cop a fix,
stick his dick in his horn with one foot,
gnaw on some fried chicken with the other.

When Roy Hargrove pushed his body through the mouth of his horn
and came out the other end,
Willie Jones the Third was flying off to Brazil on the wings of his sticks
in hopes that something would never slow him down saying, simply,
This is the way I was born.

When Roy Hargrove finished his set
he was already halfway down 7th Avenue toward the Brooklyn Bridge
before I had time to take my hands out of my eyes and grab the woman two
    seats down
who had grabbed me first, holding on for dear life, from pure joy,
and before it was over
no one knew that they had ever seen something so human
that looked so much like wind-struck dumb and perfect birds.

Raising Ali

Someone asks, "Why do you say that the opportunity
to become a great champion will never arise?"
Patterson answers, "Because you gentlemen will never let it arise."
And Floyd is talking about how to fall,
press typewriters leaking ink across his boots.

And Neruda is in the mud. He is finished.
His legs are shattered from falling.

Liston says, "If I were up there I wouldn't bite my tongue.
I would never go against my brother…"
He drinks his water in intervals of silence
so he can watch birds fly into their nests,
call for their mates.

Neruda is in the mud, fallen, completing each fall with a scream.

In each fall there is the flight of blood from his legs,
out of his knees, into the earth,
back into the world.
Neruda thinks of his brother and his brother is dead;
Neruda wants water—he is so thirsty the mud rises into his nose
and blood falls from his ears.

He believes it is time, that every fall is the last time
and that the way into the mud is the only way,
that every fall is the fall of everyman.

Liston is at Aurora Downs, an abandoned race track, skipping rope
to a record of "Night Train." He never misses a skip.
He rests and says, "Colored people
say they don't want their children to look up to me.
Well they ain't telling their children to look up to Martin Luther King,
    either."
And Patterson, with no distractions, speaks of Liston:
"Liston's confidence is on the surface. Mine is within."

Patterson goes down in one—a Liston left—
and there are no champions
and Neruda has fallen, and Neruda is in the mud.

Of Nazareth

If she comes from Ecuador to wash our floors
and her name is Nazareth
how much are we supposed to pay her
to get down on her hands and knees
with the hairnet on and a beat-up housedress from the Salvation Army?
How much is *that* worth?

There's no health insurance and no pension
and even the pigeons that fly by our window don't care
if the IRS has a bullet with her name on it,

the tiles as clean as milkweed.
So we buy her expensive soap to say *We much appreciate*
even if her child breaks a toe
and where does she catch her bus?
and how does she wander into that?

She has our keys and drops by twice a month to slick back the fridge,
wipe up the hair,
de-clog the drain
with skinny-soft fingers all the way from Honduras, maybe,
or is it Lima,
we don't know and never see her,

just leave three 20s in an envelope with her name on it,
wonder if she walks on water
and how she gets here every other Thursday
while we busy ourselves in some other kind of washed-up wandering
that belongs in a file cabinet in a green file
labeled *exile*.

Gave Up the Holocaust

Sometime at the end of the 1980s the Holocaust closed down for me.
It might have been after a conversation I had with Lia Purpura at the
    Foxhead
over a couple of Dubuque Stars
but I think it was more of a gradual finalé,
mowing lawns, leaky sinks,
a few jobs, a few cars.
And then one day it was over,
the entire fascination,
the almost desire to have been in it, part of it,
part of something.

I know a couple of people who share this feeling.
Some of them were not Jews who have since converted,
some just water their plants all day long and look at t.v.

Imagine such a desire,
to be in *that*.

It's nothing like the desire for yogurt or an afternoon by the pool,
but more, to have been in those trains, those camps,
to have been inside those ovens right before the flame was lit.
You've got to love it, such a thirst—
it's an all-out precision and attitude, it's sickness and disease.

Sometime at the end of the 1980s I had given up on being a Jew out of
    persecution
and became just a Jew.
I threw away all my books and all my pens and started fresh,
gave up my friends, my family, embraced my name.
My Holocaust fascination disappeared and I spent more time
on the bicycle, in the park,
out of love and in love,
eating pears and finally a man able to pay the bills.
I drove to New Jersey and thanked the woman who sold me a telephone.
There were windshield wipers on my car and a jack in the back.
Everything was beautiful and I still had never been to Miami.
What did it matter?
I had given up my desire for identification and slipped into the 1990s
    with new boots.

Yesterday it occurred to me that almost fifteen years have passed
since I gave up the Holocaust.
When it comes again, will I be to blame for my forgetfulness?
Do I have my passport and will it matter?

Part III

Valentine's Day

She's downtown at the bookstore—Shakespeare and Co.
I don't even know her.
She reminds me of a woman in a blue Picasso
when he could plant desire in loneliness with his spit.
Picasso—black olive eyes.
Picasso, dancing at the canvas, oils in his mouth.
And his women with spread legs facing the moon,
what did they know?
Like the bagel man on Broadway
with his truck full of bagels.
It's not June.
It's a nightmare in my head.
I watch the river rise when she dances in my belly.
I am scared to be with her;
to say: Have coffee with me before my life gets old.
It is like the wind and the wind blows hard today.
This is my whole life.
She's downtown with her books and Jewish skin from New York.
She's downtown with her torches and white sheets.
It is not even her anymore that has me obsessed.
It's that my sister was robbed on the train by boys
when the underground was a lung, black and collapsing.
Then later, said: Don't tell mother, don't tell mother anything.
It has me believing we're all Spanish muralists.
It has me believing Siqueiros was a bull.

He was insane—it's his belly, I'm convinced.

It grew from him and liberated misery.

I'm working on my own. If I get it right

I'll ride the trains forever.

If I get it right, maybe it'll lead me to her, in her bookstore,

where she talks to people about Wiesel and Wittgenstein.

I think: I'm no revolutionary though I want my own garden.

I am working on asking her to have coffee.

I am working on becoming a spiritual man

but there are so many people in New York.

So many people to watch me. So much anguish in my hands.

Ah, but this is the way it is.

My uncle says this when he speaks of his sisters

starved in the cattle cars,

"Ah, this is the way it is"—rubs his hands over his face.

And I suppose I should mention Caravaggio,

because all his boys are angels

with their small hands and rounded bellies;

because everything comes out of the darkness

and begins where the trains are welded and destroyed.

Like her, in her bookstore, where she bends in the dusk,

toward a fire in the middle of the avenue. Where she says:

"It's not the same anymore, the way the painters paint.

Nobody wants to show the body.

Nobody wants to touch themselves enough to know there is a body."

The Joy Is Everywhere

This coming from a guy who hasn't had sex in a really long time.
Well, had sex five weeks ago, once, with a woman in another state
and it was like visiting The Planetarium.
Fascinating
but you don't go back for another seven years.
And when I saw the planets this morning I was not a genius.
When I heard the birds they were swallows.
It was fifty-two degrees outside
and the joy was everywhere.
And for a long time the sex was everywhere
but seven years and five weeks have passed.
Now, there is only a bowl of apples on the counter
and the hungry body waltzing through today.
That was me in a nutshell yesterday
after the joy was in my knees
and my eye twitched for hours.
I'll tell you, not having sex is a waltz all by itself.
And then all your married friends say,
It's a draft from under the door, sex.
What do they mean?
Still, they are the married friends and ride bikes together
over big hills and into puddles
and their joy is a yellow flower everywhere.
My joy is an unbalanced checkbook,
the bills paid,

the smooth river of my ever-expanding body.
And that woman in the other state, oh,
she tasted so good and had such tropical nipples.
They were mangos or something yellow like that
when I had sex with her five weeks ago.
We won't marry, have farms,
buy cars and jewelry.
We won't talk about pianos or diapers
and we certainly won't ring doorbells.
But even when the moon goes down into nothing
there is joy everywhere
when you are not having sex
and just waltzing for hours on end around the world,
into the furniture, the moon, the space inside your own feet that is
    everything.

It Is Time for Me to Start Making Love to Joni Mitchell

It is time for me to start making love to Joni Mitchell.
It is time for me to get on a plane to Southern California and have sex
with blonde baby Joni;
the wide-eyed Joni, the one with horse breath and gangrene teeth,
the one with sunken cheeks and a forgetfulness for sin.

It is time for me to start making love with paint-brush Joni, burned out
    on smoke,
full of thistle and spruce,
walked between fourteen part harmonies heard inside sleep and out.
The Joni who wrote *Urge for Going* and *River,*
the Joni who penned *Amelia* wandering the desert with her bare feet in
    New Mexico sand
while the Zuni men wrapped themselves in her voice before paying
    homage to Elvis, Budweiser
and the exploding turquoise
that could never strip them from their grandfathers.

I would make love to the middle-aged Joni half naked, a shirt on and my
    white socks.
I would say *delicacy* and *uprising* before it was over.
Then I would open the windows like I was opening a tree
and turn to myself for affirmation and rain.

The younger Joni would be more of an issue—
fresh from strawberry eyes and blue rock—
because how do you make love to a genius at such a young age
with a face like wind,
with a whale in her spine and a humility of sky
that dances in dips and bows
then lights up the whole evening purple right before night sets in?

Yes, it is time for me to make love to Joni Mitchell,
to settle into my ways, my affairs,
eat some asparagus and bed down,
swim the sheets and smell the mushroom that is Joni,
the forest fire and old world,
make love to Joni before the fog sets in
between the eight strings of her Appalachian dulcimer already in strum.

South Going South

We were all at the same place once,
maybe it was by the river,
maybe at the rent-a-car parking lot,
standing in cold weather,
a winter sky so delicate and hard it could have been porcelain
and maybe a diamond.

We were all together with tea steaming and hot cups of coffee by the big
    stadium
in hopes the game would start soon,
hot dogs on the grill,
half naked men with beer.

It was at a roadside rest stop to pee,
all of us in one car the way traveling is a song
you make up before you can get yourself out of the backseat,
the windows broken and the cold weather inside
the cold weather a drum
between our breaths mingling in air;

all of us at the barn and taking turns with a shovel,
the cow breath and the cow shit and the cows, everywhere.
We got between them for warmth,
and then it was gone when the wind came

fifteen of us,
maybe eighteen,

in a parking lot, at a dinner party,
maybe between train stations on a train with broken brakes,
at the same place,
ducks going south,
south going south,
a light in the sky and the cold weather as fierce as a kid in a wheelchair
     with two splints;

all of us together too
and we had names that we believed in
and then that all changed and the names stayed the same
one person in a prison of grass,
another at a convenience store with six dollars,
one more telling one other where to buy cheese
and the pages all different
and the function of money
and the road split between many worlds
and the one left behind who couldn't figure it out
even with the big map in bold directives.

Hallelujah Terrible

No other man has come down that way with his foot so big
and his eyes so blue
as if the last thing he wanted to do was come down with his foot and feel
    the beginning
of earth
run through his leg.

No other man wanted to scream that way before the sun went down
and the rain began in his underwear at the foothills
opened mouth before the owl and hawk and other bird circling above
    that dead thing in roadway
called godfoot.

Who must know the pulse of two baby girls on the factory floor upset
    and upbeat
before the whistles blow sounding mmmmmmm?

Nothing else is as beautiful as the other man putting his fist through two
    planks of wood
so large the timber men come for him
for consultation on the last state of the trees.
The trees are real.
That is their state.
They holler mom.

There are no other men in the shower washing their arms
for godsakes the arms so dark there are nights coming in close
for comfort
and stars wandering past other stars looking for help.
The help is in the blood.
The blood is as you expect.
See it leak from his knuckles above the sink. Stain the sink.
So jewel-like and unlike anything
that might exist in any part of the universe swirling this way
and into corners.

No other man has blood as blue as sky in September
before the angels choke on foliage and the trees blast off
singing hallelujah hallelujah terrible terrible hallelujah.

Made of Something

I've cleaned the whole house with my feet and tongue.

Every corner is dustless.

Two years ago I rolled around parking lots naked and got gum in my hair.

I was not a Mormon or even a savage from Papua New Guinea.

I lived in a two-bedroom apartment,

wrote sordid poems,

wore the same pair of underwear three days in a row

to think for hours on the origin of starlight.

The landlord thought I smelled lavender;

my girlfriend slept with her face under my arm;

when I went to the supermarket,

the checkout girls turned up their nostrils and took me in,

all of me.

I was that rank.

At night, I let the ham burn then bathed in its grease.

It was not that I smelled,

it was that I smelled *well.*

Funky and stupid,

the way a man is supposed to smell his whole life

so his whole life he feels like

he is made of something.

Two years ago I was made of rotted herring and dung.

I welcomed the world and broke bread before noon.

But today I cleaned the house with my wet hair and my over-bent back.
There is no oil anywhere,
no caked up chowder on the sides of this fridge,
no sludge to sleep in.
I am so proud of myself
that I lean out my window to tell the world,
to call to the pregnant women walking by in their waddle,
Come on up Honies,
come spread your legs
and have your children in my germ free,
ammonia happy and amniotic home.

Moby Toby

I can hear the ocean in my empty Pellegrino bottle.
I put it up to my ear and watch my neighbor's flag fly stiff in an October
    breeze
that reminds me, the way all wind does,
of jumping the Wallkill River when I was eight.
I am not eight anymore and the pull of everything no longer feels young.
The world flies stiff and flutters in heartache and orange.
Last night my friend Lisa had her son, Tobias.
When Thad, his father, cried to me on the phone
his breakdown was as small as the world should be
in the ocean that is.

Yesterday Ishmael was one hundred and fifty years old
and in some places in New York it will take you four hours to walk half a
    block.
That's important to know when I sit down with my bowl of oats
and let myself listen to the milk.
I listen like I did when I was eight, jumping the Wallkill River,
to small stones and green moss
while the upstate wind got the best of me.

Today I hear the ocean when I stick my ear into the Pellegrino bottle.
I hear Ishmael and his locomotive voice trounced out by an exploding
    whale fin
slapping at the sea.

Once, he said, *I quietly took to the ship*. But there is quiet no more.
And I wonder if all these island cities will burn the way autumn leaves do
then turn into small particles that rise to the sky and freeze into ice.
But mostly I wonder if Toby will turn into a man who travels to
    Houston
the way he traveled out of his mom
the way his father said,
When he was born it was perfect, all those moving parts,
how could something not go wrong and then not.

And I wonder if Toby will jump the Black Creek in blue sneakers when
    he is eight
then tell his dad that a fish and an astronaut are the same thing.

Time comes inside itself and shadows the earth with children.
We travel with them, we have to,
the way everything is an ocean, a piano of oceans,
a key to melody and the sound of two voices beating forward into wind.

The New Year of Yellow

The American Bag and Burlap Company on the north side of Flatbush,
    Bergen Street,
blazed in fifteen shades of red and silver
when I walked past to buy cream cheese and *The Times,*
you back in the apartment, in the yellow-tiled shower, washing.
A crocus in the window of my head
and the whole block was fifteen centuries of quiet,
nothing hidden, my hands in pocket
and you washing under the arms, I imagined, where I had kissed you at
    three a.m.,
not imagined,
and here comes the yellow crocus to fly some sort of rendered touch
    against eyelid.
Between me and you I said good morning to two women
and an overweight man
and The American Bag and Burlap building, half gone into decay, talked
    to me
the way buildings can:
you put them up and they become something to speak of.
From across the street I did not want to be an architect and you
washed between the ridge of cheek and lip watching a living come to life
across the tile of your shower, body humming cloudlike across steam rising,
a crocus, the lilt of a crocus,
the new year of yellow between you in rest under water,
me and The American Bag and Burlap building on Bergen.

Just Born

What it's like to become forty is
that all the windows get broken
and there is no pane of glass
between me and what was me,
no buffer to stop the elephants from
crashing through;

what it's like is
that adults I knew as a kid
start to get sick with cancer and angina
while cars explode spontaneously in garages
and little dogs roll down hills
with no paws;

me, my knees drill themselves into limestone,
my bladder blows up
and the children in playgrounds
don't look like children anymore;

what it's like to turn forty is
that numbers begin to resemble lilacs
and beer becomes butane;
I am no longer a boy on a bike
or a teen with teeth marks
but rather a distant foghorn of who I used to see

when I saw myself, dead,
on the side of a road;

what it's like is:
there's a daughter in my wife's belly
and I sing in seven octaves of lullaby to her
in hopes that what she hears
will smell like honey
so that when she comes into the world,
when she begins in her new beginning
her cradle and cry,
she will explode into my forty-year-old arms
and she will be just born
then kick her legs, chew on her fist,
and go coo coo coo
peekaboo, daddy, peekaboo.

The Art of Being Backward

You have to learn things backwards.

That way you get to see the patterns in things.

That's what Gottesman told me when we sat at the desk and talked
about numbers.

But he wasn't talking about numbers, really.

He wasn't talking about x plus y or three plus four

or even integers and their place in the history of physics.

He was simply stating a fact, something he discovered in second grade

when they tried to make him memorize the multiplication table.

That was the problem, he told me, that they tried to make me memorize
the thing.

And then the birds flew out of his head

and his eyes got big

and he started to see shapes in numbers

like rectangles and squares and then circles and before he could stop

there were cubes turning into elephants and cones turning into flowers

and then three dimensional diamonds eclipsing everything he believed
about integers

and morphing into colors.

So you see, he said, I had to invert my whole way of being

because my 2nd grade teacher told me to memorize the multiplication
table

and my brain blew up.

It was like finding god for the fun of it and then making a sandwich, he
said.

A sandwich? I asked.

Yep, he said, because it all felt so natural and it wasn't even my fault.

And Gottesman has been building things ever since, from back to front,

because you have to,

because that's the way the earth is and why the trees bend and the cars
    stall.

And because one thing will always lead to another

and the milk will always be white

and numbers will always be numbers until you turn them into pants,

turn them into tomatoes,

make them whole and then divide them

so you can walk into your house at the end of the day and kiss your
    daughter

while she's in there talking to crayons about love

and not because she has no one to talk to

but just because she's simply figuring out a new way to speak

all by herself.

The Author

Rachel Putterman

MATTHEW LIPPMAN is a writer and teacher. Currently he teaches English Literature and Creative Writing at Chatham High School in upstate New York, and has been a member of the faculty, Writing Division, in Columbia University's Summer Program for High School Students, as well as an instructor at The Gotham Writers' Workshop. In 1990 he received his MFA from the Writers' Workshop at the University of Iowa and in 1997 he was granted a Masters in English Education from Teachers College, Columbia University. His poetry has been published widely in such journals as *The American Poetry Review, The Iowa Review, The Best American Poetry of 1997,* and *Tikkun.* In 1991 he was the recipient of the James Michener/Paul Engle Poetry Fellowship from the University of Iowa; in 2004 he won a New York State Foundation of the Arts grant for his fiction.